THE PERSISTENCE OF OBJECTS

THE PERSISTENCE OF OBJECTS

POEMS BY
RICHARD GARCIA

AMERICAN POETS CONTINUUM SERIES, NO. 102

BOA Editions, Ltd. ◆ Rochester, NY ◆ 2006

First Edition
06 07 08 09   7 6 5 4 3 2 1

Publications by BOA Editions, Ltd.—a not-for-profit corporation under section 501 (c) (3) of
the United States Internal Revenue Code—are made possible with the assistance of grants from
the Literature Program of the New York State Council on the Arts;
the Literature Program of the National Endowment for the Arts; the County of Monroe, NY;
the Lannan Foundation for support of the Lannan Translation Selection Series;
the Sonia Raiziss Giop Charitable Foundation; the Mary S. Mulligan Charitable Trust;
the Rochester Area Community Foundation; the Arts & Cultural Council for Greater Rochester;
the Steeple-Jack Fund; the Elizabeth F. Cheney Foundation; the Chesonis Family Foundation;
the Ames-Amzalak Memorial Trust in memory of Henry Ames, Semon Amzalak and Dan
Amzalak; and contributions from many individuals nationwide.

See Colophon on page 128 for special individual acknowledgments.

Cover Design: Steve Smock
Cover Art: "Richard's Dad" by Rose Studios
Interior Design and Composition: Richard Foerster
Manufacturing: Steve Smock, Bookmobile
BOA Logo: Mirko

Library of Congress Cataloging-in-Publication Data

Garcia, Richard, 1941–
  The persistence of objects : poems / by Richard Garcia.— 1st ed.
      p. cm.
  ISBN 1–929918–84–4 (pbk. : alk. paper)
  I. Title.

  PS3557.A71122P47 2006
  811'.54—dc22

2006006974

BOA Editions, Ltd.
Thom Ward, Editor
David Oliveiri, Chair
A. Poulin, Jr., President & Founder (1938–1996)
260 East Avenue, Rochester, NY 14604
www.boaeditions.org

For Katherine

Contents

THE PERSISTENCE OF OBJECTS

❖❖❖

THE MOON

One night the moon came into my room. It must have said something, because I sat up, startled. Who's there?

It's only me, the moon replied, Go back to sleep. I began to rise, but the moon made reassuring gestures, whispering, Sleep, sleep, it's OK.

I lay back pretending to sleep with the sheet over my face. But I left a little opening so I could keep an eye on the moon as it perused my room. Quietly, it pulled open drawers, examined pictures, touched the clothes that were thrown over a chair, read the titles of books stacked on the bureau.

Finally, I got tired of watching the moon and went back to sleep.

Then I dreamed that the moon came into my room and I sat up. Weren't you just here a moment ago? I asked the moon.

Shush, said the moon, Go back to sleep, you're dreaming.

NICK OF TIME

The demons of night were about to clamp
their star-capped teeth upon him but fortunately
he had recovered his Captain Midnight Decoder Ring

although he had thrown it away in a rage, squatting
over a sewer at Delmar and Waller when he was eight
years old, shoving it between the absolute

black grate because he could not figure out
how it worked—the outer black ring incised
with white numbers, which could revolve around

an inner circle with all the letters of the alphabet.
Although it had lain at the bottom of the sewer with rotting
newspapers, the cardboard caps from milk bottles,

shreds from an iceman's black leather shoulder apron,
a chunk of the blinders of the ragman's horse,
and tar that had been chewed and spat out by children,

although it had made its way to the ocean, still whole,
because plastic never dies, and after many years of drifting
and being lodged in crevices and tangled

in the drifting hair of weedy creatures, the ring floated
into the inner spiral staircase of a chambered nautilus.
And when the flesh of the nautilus was sucked out

by a starfish, its shell washed up on a beach
in Los Roques, Venezuela, where a child picked it up
and sold it to a tourist who gave it to a fisherman

who was the same man that so many, many years ago
had thrown the Captain Midnight Decoder Ring
into the sewer, and now it fell out on the kitchen counter

just in time to save him, because it was his birthday
and he needed to understand it, how the outer numbers
could match up to the inner letters, and how those calibrations

could create or decode any secret alphabet—how even the stars,
when they turned on their vast axis through the night,
were like the small circle of outer numbers on his ring—

and it did not frighten him that there were only a few people
on the planet who remembered Captain Midnight, Captain
Midnight, his cold Ovaltine shaker, and the secret decoder ring.

Under a Black Flag

In my *Moby Dick* Captain Ahab is Hitler.
That's why he stomps around, dragging his peg leg,
muttering about those Jews, Gypsies, mongrel intellectuals,
communists, homosexuals, and decadent artists—
they all coalesce into the image of that cursed whale, cursed
albino with the black heart, black blood, black milk of emptiness!
And the *Pequod*, the *Pequod* is Western Civilization
following the white whale through an existential darkness
of a world made lonely from the Death of God.
Hitler, poor Hitler can't find any Aryans to join his crew
so he settles for American Indians, Blacks, and Ishmael,
whom he suspects might be an Arab. Me? I'm in the book too—
Pepito the cabin boy. Being illegal, I have to sleep
down in the hold with the rats and the ballast
graveyard dirt—and I sleep well, rocked
by creaking timbers, and herds of whales singing
ghostly ululations of Ahab's death song. But my *Moby Dick*
is in a kind of eternal present. That's why Nathaniel Hawthorne
leans toward Herman Melville as they bounce along
in a horse-drawn carriage and tells him about the article he read
in the *Gazette*—a white whale often seen off the island of Mocha,
that the sailors call Mocha Dick. A white whale, festooned with lances,
ropes, harpoons—a whale that can flip a longboat, turn on the ship
and sink that too. Melville is taking notes, thinking, Mocha,
Mocha . . . he'll have to make up some other name for the whale.
Simultaneously, the *Pequod* is going down. Moby Dick,
AKA Jehovah, AKA Yahweh and other mistranslations
for that emptiness that cannot be named, swims off,
his frothy wake white as a bride's veil. Hitler shimmies up the mast,
not to save himself, but just to try and grab one last
Jewish angel out of the sky. Epilogue: the sea is quiet and rolls
on as it had a thousand years ago. Hitler drags his leg across the deck,

but you can't see him because we have all become transparent
and our ship is made of glass. We sail under a black flag with
        allegiance
to the dark matter of the universe. Hitler is at the helm.
He has set our course for the farthest archipelagoes of the Milky Way.

Self-Portrait as Goya

He stares into a small mirror and writes this down
while the glare from the ceiling light surrounds his head
and his shadowy, backlit face. The reading glasses
halfway down his nose make him look scholarly.

Removing them exposes an ancient bewilderment—
a pre-Columbian glaze in his eyes, the way the Aztecs
stared at the conquistadors, their horses, armor, wondering,
are they machines, or half men, half animal?

And like an Aztec mask that is half flesh, half bone,
one of his eyes seems to be staring inward, introspective,
morbid, turned away from the world, while the other eye
stares outward, seems positive, even friendly.

He studies his forehead with its strata of high-water marks,
insects burrowing through layers of old, rare parchment,
a pile of sheets neatly folded into compressed sleeplessness.
His left eyebrow saves him, an arch of irony.

The corner of his mouth mimics the brow but upside
down, suppressing a smile. Wait—he moves in closer to
the mirror, there is something in there, in the iris.
It is a long, dark hallway, maybe a door at the end and someone,

a thin person—is it a young woman in a slick, black raincoat?
She's nervous, perhaps a summons server, pacing back and forth
before the door, and some large, menacing thing she doesn't
seem to notice is in the hallway moving as she moves, sliding

from side to side, seeming to approach her yet coming no closer.
Now she turns and from deep within his eyes, their eyes meet.
It's just a reflection—his hand holding the pen and the paper
he writes this on. How stupid, he laughs at himself.

While the glare from the ceiling light surrounds his head
and his shadowy, backlit face like Goya's hat lined with candles.
Yes, how stupid, the shadows on the walls, they nod their heads,
the old women, the toothless men, all laughing without making a sound.

EXPLOSIONS

In Jerusalem the sky slammed shut like an enormous book.
I ran out to the balcony. A cloud, mushroom-shaped, over the
    marketplace.
Alice, my classmate, who had been running toward the market,
twisted her ankle, fell. She heard it too, but louder.

There was Harry in Da Nang—friendly fire.
A call I did not return has kept me thinking of him.

Later, I'm back in the Haight-Ashbury. By then, I knew that sound.
Heard it coming from the station as Frank, the beat cop, was lifted,
along with his heavy chair, and flung across the room.
Being so close to the window ledge, the bouquet of fence staples
    missed him.
Now he's on the way to the hospital, his hand inside his partner's
    throat
pressing down on the jugular vein.

His partner's dead, but he talks to Frank,
who hears him in his mind: Don't be afraid,
dying, it's not at all how we imagine it to be.

And then there is Aline in Beirut.
It's the eighties, there are many explosions and she's trying to take
    their picture.
Not the smoke, she tells me, but the way the air shimmers.
One night she calls during an artillery barrage—Listen, just before
    the blast,
the air chimes like frozen leaves in a breeze.

Aline at the checkpoint—a militiaman places his rifle against her
    temple.
Funny, she tells me later, My head flew up, fast, a balloon filled with
    helium,
and suddenly I was looking down at the car, the militiaman, myself,
suddenly I was looking up at my head drifting across the sky.

Aline on her knees screaming inside explosions.
Aline on the floor, it's quiet now, Hello, she says face to face
with a cockroach, Hello my friend.

Now it's Martin taking a shower—a dull thud—too close,
too loud to be anything good. Then the phone rings, but it's not
for him this time. But he can see the smoke,
and hear the sirens. He can see it on television: how we're all part
of the same explosion and everything is flung out, comes apart
into smaller and smaller pieces farther and farther apart,
even the light shattered into smoky shards.

ASHES OF ROSES

She wanted Ashes of Roses
for our bedroom walls
but I thought that was like
Dentyne chewing gum.
No, she said, Ashes of Roses.
I thought it was goodbye,
not roses but the dusty
residue of incinerated roses.
How about Barbizon, I said.
How about a tall, yellow
butterscotch coop
at the Balmoral Hotel
in Edinburgh? Now
that's something you could
dive into and come up
with a mouthful of feathers
all aflutter. No, she said, Ashes
of Roses, you know
the clinking of a tea set
on a Mexican veranda?
I thought, More like a
window in a pink stucco house,
several ventriloquists' dummies
sitting in a pile on the sill,
some with smiling faces
pressed against the glass.
No, silly, more like a piano
with the hammers wrapped
up in chamois napkins
so they barely make a sound.
You mean, like when the gamekeepers
make their rounds in the park

at three in the morning
with silencers on their sidearms
and the high fog over the city
has that sickly pink glow?
Ashes of Roses, Ashes of Roses,
not Mysteria, Hawksbill, Sachet
or Monet Lilac. I thought of the way
I could still see her against
my eyelids when I closed
my eyes. I found myself
in a garden of pewter roses,
I thought of all fall down,
I thought of roses made
of silvery ashes, roses
so beautiful that I was afraid
to even consider breathing.

THE BLUE DRESS

A woman staring up at the moon weeps
but her only tear is made of glass.
Sometimes she finds herself at a window
staring down at a blue planet

but her only tear is made of glass.
The dream of the diminishing hand
staring down at a blue planet
that is no longer her home . . .

The dream of the diminishing hand.
Oh my! The shadow is back and waiting.
It is no longer her home.
She places a blue bottle on the table.

Oh my! The shadow is back and waiting
just when you thought you were through with all that.
She places a blue bottle on the table.
She turns toward you, her blue dress shimmering.

Just when you thought you were through with all that,
martinis straight up and Schubert's *Death and the Maiden*.
She turns toward you, her blue dress shimmering.
A woman staring up at the moon weeps.

IF ONLY

Just when all lovemaking possibilities
seemed exhausted, they heard the thud
of a distant explosion, which was enough
to nudge her off the tip of the precipice
she had scaled so luxuriously up the huge bed,
as if she had toppled down a water-slide, deliciously
out of control, sideways, backwards, head over
heels and splashing into a pool, where, after
plunging and rising in a bubbly arc, she surfaced
and lay there, face down, melodramatically spread-
eagled, as if she had drowned, fooling no one—
not passersby concentrating on cotton candy,
not her lover who rolled on his back, sat up,
and wished he still smoked. He listened
to the church bells, noticing how they didn't
gong or bong but clanged as if someone
struck each bronze bell with a wooden stick,
and he heard a cacophony of roosters
not cock-a-doodling but more of a co-co-rico,
from which he surmised, correctly, that he
and his lover had slipped into a foreign country.
He sat in bed considering several words
such as: *meanwhile*. Thus something could
happen while something else also happened.
The sun was rising; meanwhile, explosions
of fireworks assisted the Virgin of Guadalupe
in her daily ascent into the vaults of heaven.
He lit an imaginary cigarette and considered
fortunately. If something unfortunate happened
like losing your passport, something good
would occur to balance the teeter-totter of fate,
like, fortunately he did not die last night

pathetically straining at stool like Elvis—
fortunately the nerve running from the top
of his head to the tip of his bowel was not
shut off like a condemned carnival ride.
Fortunately his lover was his wife and could be,
at times, whoever he wanted her to be.
Finally he settled on the phrase, *if only.*
That was a phrase he could cast into morning,
a phrase that if repeated could become pleasantly
adrift like the footsteps descending the cobblestone
path beneath the bedroom window. If only
he knew the name of those large white birds
that crossed the sky each morning, always,
it seemed, in couples, their yellow feet
tucked beneath their tails, their necks extended,
always beautifully intent on some destination.

Not His Room

A man found a black lace evening gown in his car.
He pressed it to his face; it had the scent of orange blossoms.

That night he lay awake looking down at a marble statue
that lay next to him in bed. It was a statue of a woman,

a beautiful woman, small and thin, her small breasts
lay flat, one arm was crossed over her throat.

He noticed that it was not his room.
A red velvet dress was nailed to the wall.

He got up and looked around. On the dresser
there was a display of old combs and mirrors.

He returned to bed and lay next to the statue.
He wanted to touch it, to run his hand the length

of its side, to touch each rib. But he knew
how these things went, too much willfulness

and he would not be in the room anymore.
If he were afraid, he would wake up—

he might still have the black lace evening gown,
but he would never find his way back to the room again.

Mozart's Concerto for Glass Harmonica

There you are, at the gate of the memory palace
underneath the rusted teeth of the portcullis,
your hand raised in a puzzling gesture—
is it farewell, come here, get back, no blame,
or are you just trying to hitch a ride? But I've seen
that gesture when you sleep, as if you were saying
to someone, on the one hand . . . on the other hand.
Here is a memory to store in the palace—
You and I at the circus. The arena is dark
except for one blue spotlight. In it, a clown
stands before a table. On the table an array,
crystal wine glasses filled with different levels
of water. He's dressed in white with a conical hat,
tear marks on one cheek. With a wet finger,
he plays music that was once forbidden
because it made musicians lose their minds.
There is a blank look in his eyes and he performs
perfectly, as if he were a mechanical clown.
Now look up, the lady on the trapeze
is dropping large blue crepe-paper flowers.
Maybe the palace is the size of a dollhouse
and my eye at the window is the eye of a giant.
Maybe the palace is in my chest and my heart
is beating too loud inside. I remember
when I woke but was still asleep and saw
my chest rising and falling on its own
and then I accidentally rolled out of my body
and there were two of me lying side by side.
In an alcove shaped like a scallop shell I've placed
a list of the way lovers have said goodbye.
Developer fluid heated up, passed off
as consommé, is a standout. As is GOODBYE

written in shaving cream on the dusty windows
of a row of abandoned cars in Baja. Just as I begin
to suspect what is wrong with this picture
I notice how lightly you step over the grillwork
of the oubliette, that terrible lace under which
men are forgotten. You raise your hand again
and now I understand that gesture—
it's how you erase the distant mountains,
the palace, the sky, everything.

GHAZAL OF THE LAUNDROMAT

First you'll enter, then close your eyes inside the music.
Some days some nights never die inside the music.

Why is he smiling to himself as he twirls all alone?
You might say he's climbed up high inside the music.

It was Big Mama Thornton and the Three Tons of Joy.
Tom and I snapped our fingers, alive inside the music.

Ghazal moment in the Laundromat—hum of the dryer.
A door opens, memory flies inside the music.

Blind Willie moaning at the moons in a distant galaxy.
Dark, so dark are the night cries inside the music.

Every night he played the same song on the jukebox.
Who was he fooling? Everything lies inside the music.

"Blue Monk," its angular silences opening between notes.
Me? Nursing a bourbon, just a barfly inside the music.

It goes 'round and around and it comes out here.
You can sleep without dreams, a deep sigh inside the music.

Oakland Auditorium, he throws himself off the balcony.
It's just an act, Crying Tommy Brown, crying inside the music.

Close the door behind you, Richard—come in or out.
Now that it's so easy to say goodbye inside the music.

Furry Lewis Drops in on Surrealism 101

Right now, your eleven-year-old girlfriend
is laughing in your ear while you're galloping
down Waller Street with her on your back,
and you are eleven years old too, now you're
thirty-five holding Julian in your arms,
he weighs ten pounds, and has been here
for one day if you don't count in utero
or eternity and you say, The moose is loose
and you can feel your shirt splitting open
at the chest while you're shooting
through swinging dislocates on the rings,
lucky it is summer and even your sweat
is mixed with the smell of fresh-cut grass,
lucky your sixteen-year-old girlfriend
is watching and you are sixteen too, now
you see a note pinned to a door
while on your way to a night class,
Furry Lewis visits Surrealism 101 tonight,
so you enter a dark room and Furry
limps in rather sprightly for someone
who thinks he might be ninety and
has a wooden leg, followed by a worn-out
young man from the blues festival
assigned to pick him up at the airport
two days four nightclubs six restaurants
and three parties ago and Furry plays a slow
bluesy slide-guitar rendition never
ever recorded of "Bicycle Built for Two"
and he whoops and throws his guitar
in the air and it spins three times around
before he catches it and Furry laughs to see
the currents of Katherine's hair streaming

across the pillow as if someone could copper-leaf
the wind and Van Morrison is going crazy
on a love song spitting out Meet me
at the pylons, you can meet me at the pylons,
meet me, and right now at the pylons
a bonefish picks up the fly you tied, shoots
out the length of your line and your buddy,
who you thought came to a bad end
under house arrest in Mali, smiles at you
so I won't ask what time it is now because
you're busy and anyway now will be gone
before you can answer, which is odd,
because now always seems to last forever.

QUEEN OF THE NIGHT

A woman in the eighteenth century wanted to wear the world as her dress. She slipped her feet into the ocean. That might make nice shoes and the little bit of surf at its edge was decorative. But the ocean was too cold and kept changing. She wiggled into a bush but the bush tickled.

Night came. She climbed a mountain. It was an extinct volcano and the hole on top was just her waist size. She looked good in black. Perhaps this dress was a bit formal. But she liked it.

Now she needed someone to sing her praises. She thought of the artist Turner but there was too much yellow in his paintings. Perhaps Constable. But he was more interested in cows. Then she remembered Mozart. Despite his low humor and the scatological implications of his obsession with his dear sister's bodily functions—Mozart, yes, Mozart.

He would make her dress blacker than the night and she would move slowly as mountains do, smoothly as if on tectonic rollers, vast as the world, imperial as the night. She would be a queen in Mozart's music, and the stars would be perfect accessories for her tall, silver wig.

So What

John Coltrane strode into
Milton's All Night Billiards
carrying his own pool cue
in a black leather case
like it was his saxophone.
Man, aren't you dead, I said.
Rack 'em up, he said. He broke
like the original Big Bang
and the triangle of balls
exploded across the table,
each flying into the pockets
in numerical sequence,
except for the eight ball,
which remained right where
it had been all along.
It's gonna be a long night,
I said. How do I look, boys,
he said, Dead or Alive?
He shot all night and nobody
who played him ever
got a turn. Toward dawn
he traded his cue for a broom
and shot with that,
one-handed, behind his back,
over his shoulder.
The old guys in the chairs
along the back wall
whom we called *The Banks*
ran out of money and weren't
taking any more bets. So what
if he was dead, or if he used
a mop or a straw for a cue,

or shot blindfolded . . . meanwhile
John told stories as he shot.
That Cannonball, he said,
just hated to play "All Blues" . . .
used to go to the head
and stay when it was time
for that one; me and Miles,
we'd have to go back there,
twist his arms behind his back
and drag him up to the stage.
John, I ventured, Still playing
your sax? That's a fool question,
he said, zipping up his cue case
and striding out the swinging doors,
his broad shoulders pushing
them aside with a certain authority.
He was backlit for a moment,
then disappeared into the gray haze
that passes for dawn in this part of town.

IN THE ANCIENT CITY

The fifth Beatle is bald on top but the white hair of his temples hangs down to his waist, his black leather motorcycle jacket in shreds. He stumbles between snake charmers, penitents, beggars, fakirs and Rolls Royces.

In the patchouli-scented tent he lays his offering—a small aluminum pot full of American pennies, some Mexican pesos and a couple of tokens for a parking lot in a suburb of Liverpool.

The Maharishi says, I have been waiting for you so long.

No one knows what happened, the fifth Beatle alone with the Maharishi for fifteen minutes, but it is said that he laid his head in the Holy One's lap and cried tears of joy. It is said the Maharishi pronounced him Best, most favored, whose life is epilogue, whose music shall be forever too fine to be heard.

When the fifth Beatle leaves the tent he is smiling and the crowd reaches out to touch him.

He will strip and wash his body in the Ganges. Floating corpses will burn, their ashes raining down like confetti of a single color.

THE UNEXPECTED ANSWER

In that stiff, marine evening gown
she looked like a glacier.
Her arms were signposts to a country
where one could vanish without a trace.

She mixed me a drink, a family recipe
she called an Uncle John, and the scent of it
set off small explosions in my inner ear.
It tasted oracular, ancient, then futuristic.

Two death angels strolled into the room
their dusty wings folded over their backs
like capes, although to them the room
was a vast smoky plain, perpetually black

lit up only on occasion by desire.
That was what had attracted them,
that and the industrial polka music—
chunka-boom-chunka-boom, so German.

The carpenter trying out for Soul Train
hoisted his girlfriend over his shoulder
and she slid down his back.
New Year's Eve and the night grew older.

Who invited them I wondered?
Meanwhile a part of the arctic ice shelf,
large as the state of Maine, broke off
and floated away, and I lost myself

as the recent past became the distant past.
The man I was left the party
leaving a man-shaped hole in the door
in the exact shape of my former body.

AT THE FORMOSA CAFÉ

Our booth so dark, the waitress brings a flashlight
with the menu. If I whispered
that her waist is a fragment of a statue,
still standing after some catastrophe,

would you know it's your waist I'm dreaming of?
Tell the waitress we want that bird, that one,
there in the bamboo cage, that sings so sweetly
only those songs it manages to steal.

Meanwhile the famous ones pinned to the walls,
the famous dead who sat in these same booths
know what we don't know yet—you and I—

we're going to fall down on our backs
remaining as we have fallen, wondering—
what happened to that sky we once believed in?

THE TRUTH OF MORNING

La casa en la mañana con la verdad revuelta
and the sun comes with news from the ocean.
The joggers are out in the park fighting time.
I'm up on one elbow, watching you sleep.

I won't ask why a blank canvas hangs on the wall,
or why you slept with your hand on your cheek
as if you were deep in thought. Now you're
on your back, smiling to yourself, barely breathing.

Morning opens its paper and the world starts to turn.
Do you still have a name? Birds chirp under the roof tiles.
I have hidden something for you to find with your eyes closed.

The truth of morning: our clothes piled at the foot of the bed,
my shoes by the door, pointing in opposite directions,
my wallet and keys, forgotten on the front seat of my car.

How Many

Cuantos caminos hasta llegar a un beso—
what car chases, escapes, your black dress,
thighs clenching your cello—and how did we
end up kissing under the kitchen table?

Waiting for you I grew older, as if standing
on a runway or landing dock, where shadows
twisted head-over-heels right through me
and whole cities rose and disappeared.

What dancing to Lorca *boca a boca,*
what falling cards of angels, devils, lovers—
and the wind goading us, Stand a little closer,

No, closer, the musicians sang, and the sea
surged under the pier, lifting it higher—
what Ferris wheel lights, what constellations.

RICHARD GARCIA STEALS A POEM

Sometimes you see a dog running across
the freeway, perhaps he has fallen out
of a truck, patches of his fur are scraped
raw, his eyes are wild, saliva drips
from his jaws—but look closer. It is not
a dog, it is Richard Garcia. Soggy
particles dribble from his mouth. You think
he has stolen someone's sandwich, but it
is not a sandwich, it is another poet's
poem and Richard Garcia has swallowed it.
You think you see Richard Garcia strolling
through the concourse at the airport, suitcase
suspiciously light, but he is not there,
he has slipped into the women's bathroom
where he runs alongside closed stalls, reaching
over the tops of doors, removing purses
that dangle innocently on the hooks. If
the bathroom is empty, he will steal
the toilet paper. It was Richard Garcia
who once said to his students, Never fly
downward in a dream, but that is just what
you'll have to do to reach the Museum
of Richard Garcia, experiencing a kind
of gray-out as you pass through several
floors and ceilings and then brown and then black
as you drift down observing the smashed wine
glasses, broken plates, twisted picture frames
and unreturned library books embedded
in geographical layers of earth as you descend
the well of Richard Garcia and arrive
at last in a dark hallway illuminated
only by dioramas of history and prehistory,

each containing a version of Richard Garcia.
There he is, a teenager clinging to the rear
of a streetcar in the '50s, unscrewing the taillights.
There he is, at home among saber-tooth
tigers and woolly mammoths, squat, bowlegged,
beetle-browed, dragging a huge club along
the ground. But it is not a club, it is
his college diploma. His eye is on
the workman's stepladder opened beneath
a painted cloud. He does not even know
that he stole the painted cloud from one of
his own poems. He'll steal the stepladder too.
He will fold it up and tuck it under his arm,
not even noticing that it is not a stepladder
but a primordial emblem of the letter A.

Memory

After I was born I was placed in a glass suitcase. At least that is the first thing I remember.

The suitcase was placed in an apple orchard. It was night and I was cold.

But a lady brought me a blanket and stuffed it in with me, along with some bunched-up newspapers.

Later she came back and introduced me to my father. He was the rising moon, but was stuck in the tree branches.

My sisters were twins who looked so much alike even they were unsure of who was who. I don't recall their names.

I read in the newspapers that my brothers were away at war.

We moved to a house. My mother and sisters sat in the living room. There seemed to be a secret, something wonderful, in the closet, but no one spoke about it. Inside the closet there were many small shoes. Piles and piles of small shoes. While rummaging through the shoes I found a tiny, yellow skull.

But that was long ago. Now I wake up and write in my journal. 8:00 A.M., I just woke up. A nice lady brings me coffee. 8:03, I just woke up. A nice lady brings me coffee. She says she is my wife. I like her. 8:05 . . .

Colorado

I seem to be in Colorado and Los Angeles at the same time,
bucking for a future perch as the patron saint of bilocation.
Sister Bertha's in the alley setting garbage cans on fire
Poke Rawlin's ambling toward No Problem Bridge.

Listen, I tell the punch-drunk fighter who hits me up for change,
You go around the block this way and I'll go that way panhandling,
then we'll meet in the middle and you can have the loot.
Yeah, good idea, and he goes off twitching, jabbing at his shadow.

Now Sister's doing the electric glide, not easy on concrete but she's
got the feet of Pavlova, and fingertips like the finest white asparagus.
And this muscular guy swings a pick into the Rocky Mountains,
looks at me—Man, which way is Reno?—I point west,

he heads for his car. Tonight we'll steal the pianos from the dump
and Tyke will sit in the back of the truck pounding out Rachmaninoff
'cause he's off to 'Nam in the morning, and Jolan's sex will taste I
        swear like
the Salton Sea, she should've been a surfer not a skier,

and we'll be tangled up on the floor when a horse sticks his head
in the window. She plays piano too like the last time she played
something soft on a mountaintop that was goodbye. Poke,
they call him that 'cause if you offer him a ride he says, No thanks,

I'm in a hurry. He's about eighty or so but can still be found
in the middle of a bar fight at the Red Onion. Haven't heard from
        Sister,
word is she married a Hell's Angel and got big in real estate.
I'll come back for fifteen minutes one day and sit on a rock I tried to
        blow up

in another poem. Poke, that's his arm alright, waving from a pile of
      rabbits
he had no heart to kill. Here comes the punch-drunk fighter, he made it
around the block—he's not stupid and I wasn't lying—he's got two
      dollars,
I've got a dollar sixteen, that's enough for him, he says, Thanks, see
      you later.

ME AND NASH

Nash always laughed at any kind of dark.
Just look at that stupid shadow,
he said as he displaced himself from a doorway
leaving nothing but his absence,
an almost visible impression in the air—
the Australian hat with brim turned up
on the side, the black leather vest.
That big trout we both almost caught was legendary.
Sometimes I hear its jaws clomp like wood blocks
in a quiet, lake-like movement of a symphony by Prokofiev.
Nash went fly-fishing over a puddle in the room,
talked loud in a restaurant about Silvie—I ask her
to kiss the mirror when I'm taking her from behind,
she says, Honey, I just don't love myself *that* much.
The aspen trees on the side of the road shook nervously
when we arrived, yes-no, maybe so.
Nash and I liked to stomp through the grove
pushing the most cowardly trees over.
Orlando Furioso. We liked to shoot arrows
straight up in the air, to throw boomerangs in the dark.
I don't know, Nash said, dropping his self-portrait
into an air shaft from the 17th floor of the Hotel Boston
in Caracas, where he was the only guest, It was dark,
but I do think that woman in the back of that bus
in Algiers had a penis and a vagina too.
He considered waves staircases to the underworld.
The last time I saw him was at the Aeropuerto Maiquetía,
it was full of sleepy-eyed soldiers armed with Uzis,
and we glided toward different gates along moving sidewalks
down an enormous corridor lit up by tiny constellations,
silently, like mannequins, without moving our arms or legs.

❖❖❖

A Letter, a Number, Some Punctuation

A
In the beginning
there was a ladder.
No, two people
leaning against each other,
their foreheads touching.
Between them, a book of instructions.

12
Twelve reasons
not to look his wife
of twelve years in the eye.
She sat up straight, staring
into the future. He was bent
over his plate.

(
One half of a parentheses
when she asked
Is there someone else?

The couple next to them
stopped talking, put down
their silver and waited.

Even the mariachis
stopped in mid coo-coo roo.

&
What is between a flower and a knife?
A candle, a candle is between
a flower and a knife.

)
Just what he was missing.
A moment between moments.
Part of something, but not.

Stanza break. Diversion.
Trying to cup a small flame
between his hands.

.

They say the universe began
with something as small as this.

When something ends
but you hardly notice.
Looking back, he can't remember
when it stopped, or why.

❖❖❖

THE BROCHURE

Poet heads are floating in the wilderness, their heads rising in the mist toward fir trees and pinnacles of granite. That's what it's like to be a poet. Your head fills up with something—air, helium, aether, poetic thoughts—detaches from your body, and rises toward the glaciers, not unlike the segmented tail of the pololo worm that resides in the mud on the bottom of the South China Sea. When the moon is full their tails separate from their bodies and rise to the surface to mate with all the other pololo worm tails.

Do poet heads mate with other poet heads in the clouds and then drift back down and reattach to their bodies? Do they mate with gods or goddesses by floating up and inside their togas? Maybe, maybe not, but I do know that in the brochure, poet heads are floating in the wilderness to summon poetry lovers to the poetry festival.

If you look closely, perhaps with a magnifying glass, you can see my poet body slouched in a chair on the stage of last year's poetry reading. My tiny pinhead is still attached to my body. I'm on next. It will be the most perfect reading of my life as a poet so far, so perfect my arm will fly out in a dramatic gesture and strike my water bottle. The bottle will fly off the podium as if I had flung it at the audience. But the audience will not notice, because I will catch it and put it back on the podium without missing a beat of my poem—this one, about poet heads floating in the wilderness.

Meanwhile, in the brochure, a poet is reading at the mike. I'm slouched in my chair and leaning toward my left. I seem to be pointing upward. Perhaps I'm whispering to the poet sitting next to me, voicing my concern that the parachute canopies undulating in the treetops like gigantic, striped jellyfish could be hazardous to all the poet heads floating in the wilderness.

FIGGING

Figging, I said to my lover
although she was not my lover.
It was our first date
although it was not a date,
we were just hanging out
at a bar in Hollywood
that was undergoing
a poetry slam
so I retreated to this hotel
that I keep in my mind
for just such occasions.
This time it was abandoned—
wallpaper falling off the walls.
There was still a mirror
at the end of the hallway
and I wondered what was
in the mirror when I closed
my eyes. Back at the bar,
my date placed her head
close to my chest, a move
I considered historic.
I pondered clyster, was that
what you would call
a horse thief who fobs off
decrepit Clydesdales
temporarily made frisky
by the insertion of chili powder
into their anus? Or is that merely
the technical name of that
tiny bit of debris you can never
coax into the dustpan?
Discreetly staring at the way

her dress tightened
along the small of her back,
I thought elsinoe might be
a good word for that most
intimate part of a woman's body
that can only be grubbled
when you're blindfolded.
I wondered if I should pretend
to whisper something in her ear
as an excuse to place
my face in her hair.
Should I, perhaps not.
Elsinoe: some poor Spanish
Knight of the Round Table
unable to distinguish
between that fatal yes
and the ultimate no.
So I told my date a joke
about the performance poet,
the priest and the rabbi.
She started to cry
her face in a flodder
big tears rolling
into her roast beef
sandwich and I figging well
knew for sure I would never
never leave her.

TECALI

That's when a young woman
I accidentally ogle
looks at me in disgust.

It's Tecali beach
where I sit perfectly content
and the sound of the waves
stops for a moment
that seems so long,
like when your sleeping lover
has been very silent
and you nudge her
to be sure she's alive.

Tecali, twin sister of Kali.
She does not wear a necklace of skulls
or brandish fistfuls of male genitalia.
Patron of non-dancers
and those who will die virgin.

A drink so potent, one sip
and you startle your wife
with a pathetic attempt
at the Mexican Grito.

Two sips and you find yourself
in a bathroom chasing
two strangers who are giggling,
then screaming as you sprinkle
their heads with Dutch Cleanser
and chant, *En nombre diablo*
En nombre diablo . . .

Three sips and that's you
waving to the police
from the very top
of a telephone pole.

It's La Plaza Garibaldi, a final,
rapturous battle of mariachi bands
and you are doing the dance

they call Tecali . . . Tecali of
tiny steps between one thousand
small candles placed on the flagstones—
barefoot, very drunk.

Sewers of Charleston

The usual metallic, gritty smell
she recalls from childhood
when she pressed her face
close to the grate, dispatching
her collection of rag dolls
one by one between the slats
and letting them drop; mom-
my, big sister, little sister,
papa—all gone goodbye.
Expeditus, let me tarry
no longer—her prayer
to the Patron Saint
of procrastination,
also known as Spedito.
For wasn't that how
she landed inside
this dream again?
And Carl, her lover
only when she's awake,
useless now, so she leaves him
floating dramatically prone
amid the bobbing rats.
So like Carl to exaggerate
even his own demise.
She begins the slow slosh
toward what she assumes
is morning—birds chirping
in the distance, the way
they do when first light
touches the tips of trees,
tentatively, surreptitiously,
as if they were tiny, delicate

imitations on display
in a museum of miniatures.
She emerges on the tidal flats,
lifts the hem of her white gown
amid small crabs and popping clicks
of gas escaping the mud.
From a distance she could be
a tall-necked egret stepping
ever so carefully through puddles.

CREPUSCULE IN BLUE OR GREEN

The evening is a poem extending itself across and down
the page of the sky. The sun slips tenuously into the ocean
like a squirrel stealing peanuts from the pocket of a man asleep
under a tree in a park by an airport. You can count on squirrels
to know the difference between a wallet and a bag of peanuts.
The tiny hairs inside my ears vibrate when I see you
sitting in front of the computer painting your toenails blue
or green. I get confused between blue and green
in the evening when I taste the approach of night
sliding down my skin through the forest of my arms.
Mr. Squirrel lives in a hole in a tree in Clover Park.
I should not be mistaken for this squirrel that slips
into pockets, nor am I the man under the tree who is only
pretending to be asleep although he is dreaming.
If you read this line out loud backwards you will say,
Say will you backwards loud out line this read you if,
which could cause a disruption in the syntax of the universe,
not to mention consciousness, and you'd inhale aluminum
through your eyes and be mistaken for a language poet.
Notice the way music, for instance, Monk's "Crepuscule with Nellie,"
proceeds across the evening in stately shades of gray,
with some blue or green causing you to remember someone
you've never met, standing at a window in an apartment house
you've never seen in a place you've never been, and you'll feel
a nostalgia of memory and desire. But if you're strolling in the park
you might hear the gardener, the one from Papua New Guinea,
say with disgust as he stoops behind a hedge, *Yuck, gumi bilong kok.*
and not have the slightest idea what he was talking about.
O the rubbery hammer of language, the shoes of doom and the painful
St. Sebastian pincushion knowledge that you know nothing,
nothing—the piercing vision when you smell a memory.
And the heart, the heart is not the organ of love, all it knows

is bumpa-bumpa-bump, bumpa-bumpa-bump. Give me the liver
for love and I will love you with all my liver for all my life
for I can turn myself inside out. I can be so small I can nap
curled up between your little toe, the one with the nail too small
to paint, and the one next to it that Ricky Ricardo, also known
as El Machete, likes to roll his tongue around while pretending your toes
are his harmonica. Someday, in the distant future, a holographic
image of your toes painted blue or green will be on display
in an ethnographic museum where they will be labeled incorrectly
as primitive musical instruments played by oiled squirrel worshippers
in a park near an airport. For the truth of time is in the porridge,
or as the Bible says, *Bereshit bara Elohim et hashamayin ve'et ha'arets,*
suggesting that gods and goddesses created heaven and earth together.
And the squirrel, as the sun setteth, sitteth on the cyclone fence
with his paws in prayer and sayeth amen. That's when all the cats
on the block come out to the front lawns and sit still for quite
a long while facing what remains of the sun like Egyptian statues.

MIRACLES

Miracles aimed at scattering my thoughts
act on my nerves, striking them as they fall
like shards of glass into the open maw of a grand piano,

multicolored glass, worn smooth from the ocean
and tempered into a cerulean, scarab brilliance
shot through with heat lightning.

Do not wave your arm along the perimeter
of my vision, it is the edge of my world
beyond which there be monsters.

For I am like the ancient city of Tenochtitlán
built on a lake in a land of earthquakes and volcanoes,
city otherwise known as the distant past. That past

also known as the milkman, the ice man, the grizzled
itinerant photographer with the sad pony—
and like everything else in my body, my emptiness

is called forth by miracles. You are one. How softly
you glide across faded flowers of linoleum, opening
the door for the iceman, block of winter hefted high on

his black leather shoulder apron, see how he kneels
before the icebox, knight-errant, blue bandanna
token of his lady, O sacredness of ice, glass of memory.

THE ELEMENT OF WATER

It's only a malapropism, the professor says,
but the men in the room are drowning,
hanging on to the ornate Victorian legs
of the bedpost or to staves from a tarot deck
that protrude from the tide that's rising.
And you, my dear, are smiling, your arms
behind your head. Is it that Purple Jesus
made from one part White Lightning, one
part grape Kool-Aid, one part whatever was
in your parents' liquor cabinet, that almost
makes you laugh with your eyes closed?
Like Jesus, Herr Professor walks on water.
He doesn't believe in cocktails—remembered,
stolen, or in collages. He doesn't believe
that pistachio ice cream eaten late at night
can help you swim through the bedroom
when it's finally underwater, and that you'll
be able to breathe underwater too. Last night
I held on to your thigh. I thought I was fishing.
I woke up still pulling on your thigh muscle
as if it were a rod. I got up, left the room,
turned on the light. But I could still feel the rod
in my hand, bouncing, bending, pulling—
and there was something deep beneath the carpet
with my hook in its lip, swimming away from me.

THE BLUENESS

The blueness extends from horizon to horizon
wrapping everything in blueness,
poppy fields, a prisoner hanging from his wrists
in Alabama sunshine that I heard about
on the morning news. Is there hope for us?
The phrase *Se fregó la cosa* is stuck in my brain,
and I am trying to resist the temptation
to rhyme it with Julius LaRosa, but who
would remember him? Such buttery
memories I have that dribble down the sky,
giving it a sickly green tinge like those strange
Jerusalem sunsets when we lay expertly pleasing
each other like a single serpent devouring itself.
Now the wind shakes the palm outside the window
so soothingly flapping the blueness back.
This time it's a thin almost invisible blue
just this side of whiteness, barely audible,
and I want to lie on the carpet with you listening
to whatever blue is saying now. Remember,
the first dream is what it says: the closet, the pile
of shoes and the bones you found underneath.
The hell with that. Just look at this sky will you,
how it covers us with its soft, blue fabric of illusion.

MY MOTHER AND YOUR MOTHER

My mother and your mother drinking tea in heaven—no, not heaven, but that place you go to live after you die and have acquired certain skills.

Your mother wants to take my mother to the PX to stock up on Folgers coffee, Ritz crackers and a couple of cases of gin. My mother wants to go to the new senior center because she read in the paper they'll be showing a movie with Mario Lanza. Finally they settle on Italy where your mother was happy for a while.

Your mother shows my mother the apartment where she lived, the echoing courtyard, and in between the same laundry still flapping on the line, the volcano. After a couple of cappuccinos on the Via Manzoni, your mother agrees, out of her Southern courtesy, to go with my mother to Mexico.

Today is the day she'll relive being the small girl in the white dress that hands Porfirio Díaz a bouquet of flowers. Overcome with joy, El Presidente announces that he won't run for office ever again. *¡Viva!* Hats and bullets fly through the air and my mother takes credit for starting the Mexican Revolution.

Your mother wants to go home to Charleston and eat some chess pie made out of eggs, brown sugar, and butter. Mine wants to eat those hotcakes again she had the first time she crossed the border and thought, What strange tortillas these Gringos eat. As a compromise, they come to see how we're doing in L.A.

But once here they forget why they came. My mother and your mother, on Olvera Street trying on straw hats. Your mother and my mother at the perfume counter in Bloomingdale's, spraying Chanel N° 5 on their wrists.

My mother and your mother at Musso and Frank's. Your mother is deep into her peach cobbler with vanilla ice cream. Mine is table-hopping, collecting autographs. She can't believe her luck, there's Gilbert Roland having a martini with Dolores Del Rio.

❖❖❖

MY FATHER'S FALSE TEETH

I take my dinners alone,
in my room, but I can still
hear them through the door,
my father's false teeth
clicking like a wooden gate
with a metal latch, swinging
open, swinging closed.
In a water glass at night
they float like an exhibit
in formaldehyde
of a stillborn child.
The nightlight shining
through the glass—
a spelunker's flashlight
in an underwater cave
illuminating the fossilized
toothed beak of a fierce bird
now extinct. My father's
false teeth, when he tries
to spit in the toilet, fall in.
Only my hand is small enough
to reach underwater
into the hole and pull them
out from the pipe
where they are wedged
sideways, slightly open.
Sometimes a woman expels
from her womb something
that is all hair and teeth.
George Washington
was said to always dine alone.
His teeth were made of wood,

whalebone, and mastodon ivory.
My father's false teeth, God's
first clumsy attempt at wings:
two imprints of a horse's hooves
in red clay, hinged together,
ringed with small square bones,
too heavy to ever fly.
My father's false teeth
in the click of computer keys
in the tick tick of the eucalyptus
outside the window
as it twists out of its skin
that falls on the pavement
like sheets of parchment.
A faraway splash in the middle
of the night, I sit up in bed, startled—
it was George Washington throwing
something across the Delaware,
not a coin, but his teeth.

MY FATHER'S HANDS

My father learned to roll the perfect Perfecto Garcia Cigar
when he rode with Teddy Roosevelt in Cuba.

In the fifties he was supposed to play the first Ozzie Nelson
but he got fired because he kept taking his sweater off.

He said it was too hot, and besides, he didn't speak English anyway.
I was supposed to be Ricky Nelson but my hair was too frizzy.

He once ran into Butch Cassidy, who had been a friend of his
in Venezuela, long after Butch was supposed to be dead.

This was at the World's Fair on Treasure Island in 1939.
Butch disappeared back into the crowd, becoming a rumor

and then legend. Once, while purchasing my school clothes, my father
asked me to sign for him on the department store charge account.

I refused: I didn't care if he had ridden with Teddy Roosevelt
or if it were he who had carried the famous Message from Garcia

out of the jungle rolled tightly into a rifle barrel,
or if he had knocked out the men who tried to shanghai him

on the Barbary Coast, or if he loaded up one hundred barrels
of bricks in half an hour after the 1906 earthquake in San Francisco.

His hand trembled when he scrawled his X and he didn't speak to me
for the rest of the day. Is that why my hand shakes when I sign my name?

The only kind of music he liked was martial music,
and he placed me on his shoulders so I could see the Chinatown Parade.

One day we were marching though the house
while "Stars and Stripes Forever" blared from the radio.

The war was over and he said, We won. What did we win? I asked.
He answered, We won you. To celebrate, he put on his grass skirt

from the islands and danced the hula, his hands becoming sky, then
        clouds,
then birds and rain, then a waterfall that emptied itself into the ocean.

My Grandmother's Laughter

My grandmother's laughter was an exploding plate,
the kind that the traveling salesman said
would never break, and he'd fling it against the kitchen floor
just to prove his point, and the plate would spin
making a kind of high-pitched whine.
My grandmother's laughter was like that, too; almost soundless,
like it was running out of breath, a stillness
astonished at itself, the quiet eye of a hurricane.
My grandmother's hands fluttered like pigeons
on a window ledge when I was falling asleep.
Her eyes were the color of accordion music.
She listened to *Sergeant Preston of the Yukon*,
read, over and over, *Anne of Green Gables*
and *Tarzan, King of the Jungle*.
I never saw her picture staring at me from the mantle.
Are you my grandmother? I would ask her.
Sure kid, she'd mumble, a cigar clenched between her teeth,
and then she'd hoist her shotgun up and blast
another of those unbreakable Melmac plates
that I would throw up in the air into smithereens.
Fuchi, that stinks, she would say
when she stuck her head in the kitchen
where my mother was cooking menudo, *huele feo*.
Because she always told the truth her shins never hurt.
She told me she could ask a question of her special spirit
and an image of the answer would appear in a bubble of light.
She said that President Truman was an estupid son-of-a-bitchie.
My grandmother only read newspapers of the future.
Sometimes she made me so happy, I had nightmares to compensate.
She would walk into my dreams and sell me magazine subscriptions—
me, known as El Diablo, the one who spits in the mirror,
who cried in the womb, who fathered his own grandmother,

he of the silent fire escapes and forensic closet dust.
Looking up from the Ouija board, she leaned over
and whispered in my ear, You will have no descendants
and be a disgrace to your many grandchildren.
Ani routsay ooga, I answered, not knowing
that I had just asked for cake in the language of Jesus.
Only I could break the unbreakable plates without a shotgun.
That is why the plates spoke to me. You will never
have a grandmother they said. It's true,
my grandmother added, blasting another plate
out of the sky. It was blue, and pieces of it rained down on me
like pieces of an angel, some beautiful, goddamned angel, shot out of
     the sky.

AN OLD PHOTOGRAPH OF MY FATHER
DRESSED AS A COWBOY

He has furry chaps made of buffalo hide
      and drawn his six-gun so fast,
          you'd think he has not moved at all

or that maybe he is a statue.
      Sometimes, when we need water,
          he shoots into a cloud and it rains.

He does this a little too often
      and we have to turn our wagon
          into a sailboat. His sidekick Tito

has to grab his arm and pull it down,
      to discourage him from filling whole herds
          of woolly clouds full of holes.

At night we sit
      around the fire and my father
          tells us all about

his many adventures. Like the time
      when, riding with his friends,
          they saw the transparent lady

beckoning from the crossroads,
      and their horses reared up,
          turned and galloped away;

the gunfight on the isle
      of Puerto Rico in the middle
          of the hurricane, and how his bullets

were flung by the wind
    right back into his own gun
        and out again. Meanwhile

the Indians, Cheyenne,
    Arapaho, and Sioux,
        who are sneaking up on us,

sit down and listen—
    munching popcorn in the dark
        as if they were at the movies.

ADAM AND EVE'S DOG

Not many people know it but Adam and Eve had a dog.
Its name was Kelev Reeshon, which means, first dog.
Some scholars say it had green fur and ate only plants
and grasses, and that is why some dogs still like to eat grass.
Some say it had pink skin like the Mexican hairless dog.
Others say it was male, some female, or that it was androgynous
like the angels or the present day hyena. Rabbi Peretz,
a medieval cabalist in Barcelona, thought it was a black dog
and that it could see the angels which were everywhere
in the garden, although Adam and Eve could not see them.
He writes in his book of mystical dream meditations,
HaSefer Halom, that Kelev tried to help Adam and Eve
see the angels by pointing at them with its nose, aligning
its tail in a straight line with its back and raising one paw.
But Adam and Eve thought Kelev was pointing at the birds.
All scholars agree that it had a white tip on its tail,
and that it was a small dog. Sometimes you see
paintings of Eve standing next to a tree holding an apple.
The misinterpretation of this iconography gave birth
to the legend of the forbidden fruit and the fall from grace.
Actually, it was not an apple, but Kelev's ball, and Eve
was about to throw it. One day, although there were no
days or nights as we know them, she threw the ball
right out of the garden. Kelev ran after it and did not return.
Adam and Eve missed their dog, but were afraid to leave
the garden. It was misty and dark outside the garden.
They could hear Kelev barking, always farther and farther
away, its bark echoing as if there were two dogs barking.
Finally, they could stand it no longer, and they gathered
Kelev's bed of large leaves and exited the garden.
They were holding the leaves in front of their bodies.
Although they could not see it, an angel followed,

trying to light up the way with a flaming sword.
And the earth was without form outside the garden.
Everything was gray and without shape or outline
because nothing outside the garden had a name. Slowly,
they advanced toward the sound of barking,
Holding each other, holding their dog's bed against their bodies.
Eventually they made out something small and white,
swinging from side to side; it seemed to be leading them
through the mist into a world that was becoming more visible.
Now there were trees, and beneath their feet, there was a path.

THE PEACEABLE KINGDOM

I wish I could write a poem about Squanto—
Squanto at our house for Thanksgiving
back in the fifties when I was a child, and all
of the family was still alive, younger, and together.
In the poem I'd introduce Squanto to my father,
John Garcia, former chef for the Matson Lines.
Thanksgiving was the one day of the year
he would cook at home. He'd adjust his chef's hat
at a cocky angle, cinch his apron, and while sharpening
his knives, ban my mother and sisters from the kitchen.
Only men allowed, just me, my brothers and cousins,
and, in this poem, Squanto, too. After all, hadn't they
both sailed the world's oceans? My father had seen things,
he always said, that a man should not see. What things,
I wondered? The child prostitutes of Manila? The public
sexual dance called "Toro"? Beheadings in Sumatra
or the slow Chinese execution by dismemberment
called "The Torture of the One Hundred Pieces"?
Squanto had seen a lot too—kidnapped twice,
taken, like Pocahontas, to London, but unlike her
he made it back somehow. Later, tricked into boarding
a ship in the harbor, he was shanghaied to Spain,
escaped, and managed to come home from that too,
only to find his entire tribe had died from the plague.
In the poem, Squanto and my father get along;
after all, both men spoke English and Spanish.
Squanto would make the pumpkin pies.
Maybe, if he comes into the poem a couple of days
early, I can take him to school and he can be
in the Thanksgiving play we have to put on.
Take that, Miss Kapelhaus!—my third-grade teacher
who thought I was a complete idiot. Who didn't

believe I could read. Who couldn't tell me and Juan
and Carlos apart. Maybe she'll think Squanto
is the fourth Mexican at Dudly Stone Elementary.
At dinner we'll put three long tables together.
My cousins will be swinging from the lamps, sliding
down the banisters, and bouncing off the couch.
Just like the first Thanksgiving, Squanto will say,
Those Puritan kids were pretty wild too.
In this poem I want to write, Squanto tells stories
about the Puritans. How surprised they were
to be greeted by an Indian in the Queen's English.
Maybe he'll joke and tell us his first words to them
were "How" or "Kemo Sabi." Maybe he will tell us
he waved in the Mayflower like a parking attendant
saying, Easy now, watch out for that rock. We'll laugh,
careful not to ask him about the second Thanksgiving.
That'll be something he does not want to talk about
in this poem—blood seeping into the snow, crows
dipping deep into the hole that a blunderbuss makes
in a man's back. No, in this poem we'll just talk about
that first Thanksgiving that began a future
that never was. We'll even have our picture taken,
all of us around the table, our dogs, my Cousin Bob
down on one knee, me reading this poem out loud
like a proclamation. I'll add a lion, a tiger, some oxen
and cows, and I'll put my baby niece and nephew
sitting in front—The Peaceable Kingdom. We'll praise
and be thankful that time doesn't exist in this poem.
After dessert my father and Squanto will sit, smoking
big Indian cigars, swapping tales—abductions,
imprisonment, bloody mayhem, escapes, and
thankfulness for safe returns from the high seas.

PONCE DE LEÓN AND THE TEN MILKSHAKES

My father claimed that his side of the family is descended from Ponce de León. That would explain why the men in our family have always been considered immature.

Ponce de León's birth: No one knows how or where or when Ponce de León was born. But it is said that he cried in the womb. Those who cry in the womb are sometimes able to know the future.

That is why members of my family sometimes know what is going to happen. When I was nine I knew days in advance that I would win a ham playing roulette at the Saint Agnes Church Easter Fair.

Why was he called Ponce de León? Would it not have been better to be roar of the lion, or claws of the lion? My father said it was because he could eat as much of anything as he wanted and his stomach would not be upset, hence, belly of the lion.

Even as a child Ponce de León knew that he would do something no one else had done, some feat or adventure that would make him legendary. When I was ten years old I knew that I would be famous for drinking ten milkshakes.

I announced to my friends, I can drink ten milkshakes! This was way back in the nineteen fifties when milkshakes were milkshakes. The challenge was accepted. Chocolate, vanilla, strawberry—each cold chrome canister filling three tall glasses with a little left over. I drank that too.

Historians have written that Ponce de León was not looking for the Fountain of Youth but for natives to kidnap and sell as slaves. My friends thought that I could never drink ten milkshakes.

Because I am descended from Ponce de León, I knew I would drink nine milkshakes and that the waitress and my friends would plead with me to stop before I exploded, right there at the counter of Glendell's Sweet Shop.

Historians have doubted that Ponce de León ever found the Fountain of Youth. No one doubted I could have drunk that tenth milkshake. Not my friends who carried me home, held above their heads like a hero of old, not my father when he saw them carry me up the stairs with milkshake dribbling down my chin. He had known that I would be carried home by my friends that day and was there to greet us.

Ponce de León! he exclaimed in triumph, pounding his stomach with his fist, Ponce de León!

Could Ponce de León have drunk all he wanted from the Fountain of Youth and never gotten full? Could Ponce de León have drunk ten milkshakes? Ponce de León's death: nothing is known of Ponce de León's death.

THE BOOK SIGNING

It was Pablo Neruda that made me
sign your copy of my book, "Later, Baby."
Possessed by his spirit I had an urge
to kiss your muscular, surf-slicing arms.

I was not afraid of the waves crashing
over you as you leaned into danger
so I came up behind you and wrapped my arms
around your waist. Pablo Neruda shouted

Take her! I pulled you away from the crumbling
edge of the stage that had become a precipice.
Why? Because he had stolen his own name—

because he knew I once dove to the bottom
of a poem even though I could barely swim,
just to steal a lovely hand made of plaster.

❖❖❖

AUTUMN

Both lying on our sides, making love in
spoon position when she's startled, What's that?
She means the enormous ship passing before you—
maybe not that large, is it a freighter

or a passenger ship? But it seems huge in the dark
and it's so close. That's a poem you say, D. H.
Lawrence—Have you built your ship of death,
have you? O build your ship of death,

for you will need it. Right here it would be good
if there were a small orchestra on board, you'd hear
them and say to her, That piece is called Autumn,

that's what the brave musicians played as the *Titanic*
went under—and then you could name this poem "Autumn."
But no, the ship is silent, its white lights glow in the darkness.

THE VIOLET VALE

Anne of Green Gables would often go to her favorite spot in the valley accompanied by her imaginary friend. She called it The Violet Vale, although there were no violets there. Her imaginary friend, Chimon, wore a Japanese kimono, and often said things like, These violets infuse the vale with the scent of sunrise.

Anne disagreed. There are no violets here, and you, my friend, do not exist.

But *you*, Dear Anne, he replied as gently as he could, are *my* imaginary friend. He was a monk in faraway Japan, and whenever he reached what his master called the traveling stage in his meditation his astral body would float to England and he would visit Anne of Green Gables.

But what can we call the violets, Anne wanted to know, as she lifted Chimon's favorite teacup out of her basket, If there are no violets?

Chimon, who was about to open his eyes in Japan and was already drifting back to his physical body, answered, Violets. And he heard the word flitting about frantically, as if it were lost, cut off, like the echo of a bell that could not return to its source.

THE PERSISTENCE OF OBJECTS

They just lie there, lacking any concept
of "in the way" or "move over." Space tightens
around them and if you move one,
like the box on your desk that holds pens,
absence pours into the hole it leaves
until the universe readjusts itself
like someone slipping a burden
from one hand to the other.
Even time avoids objects, distorting itself
in an effort to get around them
the way you will twist and contract
as you slip between passengers
on a crowded train. Maybe you're fumbling
through a pile of books and papers
looking for a Post-it and you come up
with a slide, hold it to the light and peer
through a tunnel into a room forty years ago,
it's New Year's Eve and Rhonda's head
is on your shoulder, your hair is combed
into three cliffs, a wave and a plateau,
she's wearing her poodle skirt and saddle shoes,
and you want to throw it away to get in bed
to just lie there thinking that you too
are an object, like that small leather notebook
in a drawer somewhere with the gold pencil
attached to it that your married lover
placed under your windshield wiper
on Valentine's day fifteen years ago,
like the smooth round black stone
you picked up on the beach in Wisconsin
while walking with your first wife.
It was one of those days when the wind

bends the grasses but not too much
and the sky looks like a child's drawing
on a refrigerator. You knelt and picked up
the stone. You could have skipped it against
the surface of the gigantic lake and let it sink
into forgetfulness, but instead you placed it
in your pocket. Sometimes you find it in the closet
or you feel it in the dark, cool against your bare foot
as you stumble across your office in the middle
of the night and you marvel at its persistence,
how it insists on its right to lie on your carpet,
to make you go around it or push it aside.

A Thing You Did Not Do

A thing you did not do is a pickpocket. A nondescript white guy in a secondhand powder-blue suit. Most people wouldn't notice him but you do. It's that prison saunter, even in a crowd. Slowdrag's a giveaway.

Another thing you did not do climbs in your window at three in the morning, always at three in the morning, ¡ai! She's wearing a brown suede jacket and has a green and yellow plastic bracelet on her wrist.

She sits in a chair, slightly bouncing and swaying as if she's on a bus, waiting, hoping you'll speak to her before her stop. She thinks she'll never see you again. Wrong. Here she is, sitting by your bedside at three in the morning watching you sleep.

That first thing you did not do is getting a haircut. He's talking up the barber, establishing eye contact, rapport. You know he's going to do *Oh I left my wallet in the car be right back.* Even if you could alert the barber, he wouldn't believe you. He likes the thing you did not do. He's telling him a joke in Spanish, which the thing you did not do pretends to understand.

Perhaps it's a small thing you did not do. You meant to, and mentioned it to friends, Why bother, they said, and you listened.

A small thing someone else did not do calls you on the phone. Apparently she has mistaken you for someone else with the same name. You explain she has the right name, but the wrong person. That's all right, she says, and you continue talking late into the night.

❖❖❖

HOLDING CELL

They have taken your shoelaces, belt, and keys.
Five hours or more—how long can they keep you here?
You sit with your arms wrapped around your knees.

You were shaving, the door opened as in a breeze,
and a cop, younger than you, nervous, stood there.
They've taken your shoelaces, belt, and keys.

Now it's you that's nervous, ill at ease—
your name on a warrant, a misunderstanding, an error?
You sit with your arms wrapped around your knees.

What's keeping you here, bad luck, legalese?
Everything's white and naked in the caged bulb's glare.
They've taken your shoelaces, belt, and keys.

No one to talk to, it's yourself that you tease,
Keep a hold of yourself in the holding cell. Wait, stare,
your arms wrapped around your knees.

Half-shaved, nothing to cinch your faded dungarees,
you feel like an old man with nothing left to spare.
They have taken your shoelaces, belt, and keys.
You sit with your arms wrapped around your knees.

OBJECTS ON A GLASS TABLE

The chocolates in their narrow box shall be my desires all lined up ready to come when called upon. The checks in a pile are letters you did not write, or the letters that you imagine when you think of me.

There is a bit of ribbon trying to be a cactus dusted with snow, in other words you—cold, forbidden, and forbidding.

If you walked, carefully, across the lake of glass, would you be afraid of falling? Or would you think you were flying, following the beacons of your hands over the parapets of envelopes and the crushed tinsel of cathedrals?

Speaking of flying, the glass of water trembles with excitement, the way an airplane shakes itself off the ground.

Trembles, then is still, the way the shadow of the plane you took dragged itself over clouds, then buildings, flitted over the tarmac, then came to rest beside you.

SHOES

You can tie knots in the laces to remind you of something, for instance, that your shoes are like holes and their heels are the shape of gravestones.

From a distance, one could be mistaken for a phone while you hold it to your ear in an effort to appear occupied when all you're doing is sitting on a stump.

If they are attractive wing-tipped Florsheims with elaborate stitching, or velvety Italian loafers made of unborn calf leather, the kind James Dean wore in part two of *Giant*, they would be fought over by your jailers.

In a dream you hear something, look up, your shoes are flying upside down, their laces brushing against your forehead, plastic tips clicking against your glasses.

If your wife has just mopped the vestibule you have to take them off before you enter, and place them on the stoop, as if they were small, obedient but useless guard dogs.

What can you say to them at times like this except Wait for me, or Don't let yourselves get stolen by a wild animal.

Whereas, they moan and complain more than your feet: You leave us out here alone in the cold. You always put the other one on first. When you want to make love you forget how our laces work, yank us off, throw us anywhere—blah-blah and so on, their tongues lolling.

CONSIDERING YOUR HAND

Look at it joined to its twin in prayer, so innocent, all church and steeple. But you knew a woman with the thumb of a murderer.

Lying open, it is so Buddha-like in supplication, submission. A model of a country where pale brown rivers lie still in crevasses. From this height you can't tell if they are ice or silt, or if they are the remains of rivers long since extinguished.

Falling toward your hand you are not afraid, it looks so friendly—hills, rolling grass, snow, sand, moraines dragging trains of gravel.

It remembers when you were in love with a curved knife, or was it exploding shards of glass that embedded themselves in paint, making a kitchen sparkle? Now all that is left of that is a V-shaped flight of geese cruising over the fabled mound of Venus on their way to someplace else.

Your hand has a life different than yours. You don't trust it, you put it in your pocket if there is something to steal or a complete stranger to fondle in the cafeteria line. Its proudest moment: stealing a pencil from a cop during a strip-search. Not too many hands can steal when they are naked.

No one has ever believed you when you explain that your hand is a sentient being. It was not your fault when you ran over your ex-girlfriend. You watched your hand pull the throttle—really she was fine once they got your motorcycle off her chest.

What if you woke and someone else's hand was attached to your wrist? You know, how when your hand is asleep but you are not? When you touch your hand, it does not know you anymore.

Angel Face

Looking into her eyes was like playing with matches in a gas-filled room. You'd just as well try making love to an angel. Driving an ambulance, you see a lot. One afternoon I retrieved a blonde's head from a culvert.

But nothing got me ready for Diane Tremayne. Not even all those other Dianes and Dianas in my life, so many I referred to them by number—Diane #1, Diane #2, a Dina, a Dinah, a Dee Dee. I see now they were practice, maybe warnings.

Diane Tremayne. She'd come toward you looking up with those eyes so innocent, in her pink bathrobe with the shoulder pads and tiny waist cinched tight, and next thing you know you're bent over her while she's arched backward above her husband's semiconscious body in the back of your ambulance.

You've turned off the radio, and she's got the keys anyway. You don't tell her that her face is doing this changing thing, changing from one face to another, into the faces of all the other Dianes you've known. Like she really is an angel, one of those dark ones who can pull you down through the sheets and you're falling through icy clouds.

DARK PASSAGE

The lines of the poem I am trying to write get longer and longer, until they become a train and I am left alone on the platform, catching a glimpse of the lights on the caboose just as they disappear into a tunnel.

Seeming to feel sorry for me, my computer says, Looks like you're writing a letter, would you like some help? Now someone in the house next door is playing show tunes on the piano. I think it is a man. He is small, portly, harmless looking, but actually he is here in San Miguel de Allende hiding out from gangsters whose money he stole.

"I Only Have Eyes for You" . . . "September Song" . . . "The Way You Look Tonight."

Someone has come to the piano player's door. He hands a servant a note. The servant carries it to the piano player and the music stops. The note says, You have something that belongs to me.

And now my computer is angry. It says I have performed an illegal operation. Like a drunken plastic surgeon in a back alley in Tijuana, I have altered the piano player's appearance. He's hiding out at Tia Lucha's. Pianoless. His face wrapped in bandages. He's sitting in the dark remembering my face blurring above his, my breath smelling of tequila, my shaking hands.

Opportunities

Your best friend's in the movies—there he is,
in *Escape from Alcatraz* shoveling
prison slop into his face; wary, calm,
yet capable of leaping up and scooping
out a guard's eyeball with his spoon.
He's good, so good they want to give him
a speaking part, his name in the credits—
other acting jobs to follow. But no,
your best friend can't stand being in a cell,
even in a movie. Besides, he's hungry,
maybe all that fake prison chow made him
salivate. He eats lunch with Clint Eastwood
while some other actor gets to rattle
a tin cup against the bars and scream, I'm
going crazy in here! and get his name
on the credits and become famous. Clint
is soft spoken, your friend will say later.
He's a vegetarian, he likes jazz.
And the temp that worked at the desk next
to yours all summer, the one whose high heels
were a couple of sizes too big and who clomped
around and whom you called Minnie Mouse,
she's in the movies too. All summer
you ignored her but now on her last day
the whole office, the social workers and
even the priest—you're all watching the temp
in a video of her movie. It's black and white,
lots of cars in the night and stiffs rolling
out of cars into alleys. Now a detective
is leaning back in a chair chewing on
a toothpick, he's wearing his fedora,
and the temp—here she is standing right

next to you, and there she is in the movie.
Her hair is blacker and she doesn't have
those glasses on, she's wearing a black skirt
which she has pulled up and she's pressing
it against her hips with her forearms
and while the detective is leaning back
in his chair eyeing her she is slowly,
ever so slowly slipping her black panties
off with little rolling motions of her wrists
in what must be the longest single-take-
slipping-panties-off scene in movie history
and suddenly you look at the temp and
you can smell her perfume, it's Jovan Musk,
and you're thinking maybe you could have been
a little friendlier to the temp, maybe
you could have impressed her with your knowledge
that musk is scraped from the bloated scrotum
of the rutting musk deer in Central Asia,
maybe you could have helped her rehearse
during lunch break, maybe you could have been
the detective. But wait a minute. Now
you remember as you're writing this down,
your best friend was in jail, where he fell
in with some toughs and they planned an escape.
It was even his idea. But when the time came,
he stayed back. Maybe he was hungry,
deciding to eat lunch rather than escape.
And you—you were in jail too, Brooklyn
Detention House, maximum security,
and you did escape—your proudest moment,
for once you didn't hold back, you acted,
just like a movie—shimmying up a drainpipe
as you heard the cops below cursing
and kicking in the door to their bathroom.
And later, after you're recaptured,

and your best friend gets his childhood buddy
to ask his parents to help with your bail—
we'll have to try and get a young version
of Robert De Niro to play him because it was
Robert De Niro, "Bobby," as he was called then.
Just home from acting school, How about it
Mom? he said, I hear this guy's a poet, all
we need is five hundred bucks . . . But now
it's late night TV and there is your friend
hopping a freight car with Woody Guthrie
in *Bound for Glory*, it makes you remember
how you and your friend did hop a freight car
after missing several chances by waiting
too long, after scampering onto a flatcar
that was suddenly disconnected and rolled
slowly to an embarrassing stop in
an empty freight yard. After letting a whole
train go by, in the last moment you caught
the caboose and the two of you sat there
on the stoop, it was cold, sparks were rising
into the dark above you, and a railroad man—
who can we get to play him?—stepped out,
handing each of you a cup of hot, strong coffee.

FUNHOUSE MIRROR

I'm just a rube
three feet tall
five feet wide.
Strands of string
brush against my forehead.
Laughing Sal
rocks back and forth
in the window
her crazy laughter
like a dark room
made of glass
shattered by gunfire.
A little man smaller
than me appears
claiming to be the Duende.
Yo soy El Duende.
He leans his face
against my elbow—
Your bones, he says,
smell of blood. *Sangre,*
sniff, sniff—*sangre.*
This causes my body
to adopt the sinuousness
of the sigmoid curve.
At least I can't be accused
of failure to waver
as I slither down
a spiral staircase
and into the mirror,
a red box with pathetic
silver trim. No sound
as the lid slams shut.

I am told that
its yellow lights
have come alive
flashing sequentially
humming in their fashion.

CALCUTTA

Devila, the eunuch, stared into tea leaves at the bottom
of my cup, looked up, batted his large, sad eyelashes
and said, Two women are plotting against you.
Sure, I thought, Tell me something I don't know.
One's got lips like sapphires in monsoon rain.
The other's got a gun. Which is more deadly?
I should've slipped myself a Mickey.
But there I was stuck in Calcutta with Virginia Moore
and her alter ego, whom she referred to as My sister,
Lakshmi. Virginia was a red dress overripe with trouble
and Lakshmi was a suitcase full of stolen jewels.
Virginia counted on her beauty with guys like me—
even ones she was going to kill—a beat-up pilot,
a beat-up plane and a license revoked years ago,
stranded in a hellhole so long I was beginning to like
the mooshed-up chapatis they called food around here,
those potatoes and lentils beaten to a pulp.
Take us with you, she pleaded, Me and Lakshmi.
I knew, when I got them across the border, I'd have to pay
double rupees for those double kisses. The hidden riptides
in Lakshmi's dark eyes and the pal named Roscoe
Virginia kept under her pillow. Take me, Lakshmi whispered
in my ear, as she gave me a private tour of her sacred gardens.
I can pluck a lotus from your clenched teeth
with any part of my body. Probably true, I thought,
remembering what Devila always said,
Man who trust woman walk on duckweed over pond.
If Virginia and Lakshmi were two people, who was I?
Alan Ladd, pilot on the skids, or his sidekick,
William Bendix? If I was Alan Ladd I'd have to stand
on a milk crate just to get my face in proximity to Virginia's
nirvana tits. If I were William Bendix, I'd always be

the sidekick, always end up married to Lakshmi,
who although she looked exotic—skin of ripe tamarind,
golden earrings bouncing against her gazelle throat,
was just a stay-at-home at heart, or a business major
on vacation who could calculate each of my failings
with her abacus mind. At least if I'm the sidekick,
I'd have a chance of making it back to the states.
Hell, it's the fifties, Lakshmi can change her name to Shirley.
Me, I'll spend my days meditating in the backyard hammock,
beer, smoke rings, the Fourth of July, the life of Riley.
But there I was, having a midnight meal with Virginia.
Devila is dying, I said. These strawberries are delicious,
she said, pushing one into my mouth with her fingertips.

PAVILIONS MOTEL

He heard the word *gobslip* in his head. What was that? Perhaps it was what he spat out when he was angry. A blustery anger, the kind that made him pace back and forth in room sixteen of Pavilions Motel. There was just one thin blanket on the bed, no soap, and a roll of toilet paper that was almost used up. There was mold inside the medicine cabinet. He pulled a drawer out of the bureau and it fell to pieces in his hands. He saw that someone had written on the inside of the drawer with black marker the phrase, *Fuck me, Curtis.*

He stood outside in the parking lot looking up at the clouds. It seemed that they were angry too. *¡Hoy! ¡Hoy!* they would shout, streaming by in sped-up time. Another word he did not know the meaning of. He pretended to ignore them, but really he wanted to join them. To be a drover of clouds sitting on a gray, slightly cantankerous cloud, to crack a fine, stiletto-thin whip of rain over their cloudy heads.

But if he were to call out to them would they listen? Or did he read this in a poem he read once a long time ago? How clouds strolled together by the ocean two by two, speaking to each other, but how they would never, never speak to him.

Back inside he lay down in the dark and covered himself with his jacket. He closed his eyes and saw that the entire planet had become Pavilions Motel. The earth was not round anymore, but more like a glowing jukebox floating through black space. There were shiny terraces, and whole continents were made of multicolored plastic lit up from the inside. The sound of someone dipping a bucket into the ice machine became raucous saxophone music. He thought, Sam Butera on sax. He thought, Maybe I am Curtis.

❖ ❖ ❖

HOLLYWOOD

This poem is not about itself, not about sailing
in a paper boat across a sea of intransitive verbs.
This poem does not know what an intransitive verb is.
It's not about sailing across your belly with my tongue
until I bump into the silver ring in your navel.
This poem is trying not to think about the silver ring
in your navel, not to think of its tiny skull face
that I can only see if I leave my glasses on.
It's diving underwater with open eyes.
It's about pulling myself rung by rung down
the page until I am sitting on the bottom of a swimming pool
but still able to breathe. The pool must be in Hollywood
because here come Esther Williams and Fernando Lamas
in the prime of their lives swimming side by side
barely disturbing the surface of the pool—
backstroke, butterfly, crawl, and suddenly the pool
is lined with towers of spray and scissoring ladies
of the aquacade in white bathing suits, all of them hanging on
to the edge of the pool, each with one leg in the air, foot arched,
toes pointed—a good time for you and me to slip away
barely disturbing the surface of this poem,
leaving the scratch, scratch of pen against paper far behind us
and there is only the sound of our breathing—
and with my face pressed into your hair, I ask you,
What do you call this kind of poem?
Ask me about the ocean, you answer, I don't know about pools.

DREAMING OF SHEENA

The sun wiped out the night like an eraser.
It was a morning fit for pancakes
but my lucidity found no outlet.
So I went back to my dream, a groovy
dream of love, adventure, and terrorism
and Sheena of the Jungle in her underwear.

Sheena had skimpy, leopard-skin underwear.
Her thonged behind emptied my mind like an eraser.
Then, out of frustration, I became a terrorist
with explosives disguised as pancakes
and plastiques in my shoes that were groovy.
My mission: blow up the Eddie Bauer Outlet.

Or was it the Citadel or the Desert Hills Outlet?
I had ammunition stashed in my underwear.
It made me walk bowlegged but I felt groovy.
After a series of explosions I craved pancakes.
But they tasted like warmed-over pencil erasers.
I wanted to dream of love, not terrorism.

Or was dreaming of love a kind of terrorism?
But dreams of love were not the way out.
Let me find a woman with the scent of pancakes.
I searched for a phone number over and under.
Where could it be, I hope I didn't erase
her number from existence. Then—groovy

and cool, I found it and let me repeat, groovy!
I tried to focus and dial but I was in terror.
Isms of doubt crossed my heart like erasers

on a blackboard. Would I find an outlet
for my jungle passion sniffing her underwear?
Or was she really just ugly under her pancake

makeup? Could I be the one to butter her pancakes?
May her thighs snap shut on me! Here follow groovy
fantasics of Sheena underwater in her underwear,
Sheena with knife between teeth, Sheena fights terrorism,
while I toss and turn, wishing for an outlet—
here follow galloping zebras striped black and white like erasers.

Would I wake to pancakes or love like terrorism?
Or might I wake yelling groovy or take me to the outlet!
May our underwear spin together or from my dreams erase her.

NOT BAD FOR A HERMAPHRODITE

The poem was scrambled during transmission.
Previously, it had been tied to a gate and disemboweled.
Some said it was a hermaphrodite
whose secret name was suspected of being an anagram
of a supernatural being, a quadriplegic
God, fond of anyone who dressed Goth.

The poem could sing the entire libretto of *Faust* in Goth.
It could hum like a cherry V8 transmission
in a loaded '56 Chevy; it was, however, quadriplegic,
and four of its stanzas were immobile, disemboweled
and deveined. It had chutzpah and a gram
of old-fashioned moxie, not bad for a hermaphrodite.

In fact, it was titled "Not Bad for a Hermaphrodite."
In days of old it was chanted by drunken Goths
who thought its power was that it was an anagram
of something really important but lost in transmission.
The true truth of the universe unfortunately disemboweled,
disheveled, and discarded on the road like a quadriplegic

marauder who couldn't admit he was quadriplegic.
Why was the poem hermaphroditic?
Because it was male and female, disemboweled,
held up by exterior struts of language like a Gothic
cathedral, for it needed no vowels, it was pure transmission
and was just one word of an infinite license plate anagram.

Or was it one word of an orgasmic anagram?
The poet was fabled as a great lover, although quadriplegic.
The attention of his tongue, it was said, was direct transmission

to goddess-hood, pleasures beyond what contortionist hermaphrodites
strapped to vibrating washing machines during spin cycle by soapy Goths
could ever know, even if all inhibitions were disemboweled.

The poem would survive, even disemboweled,
for an alphabet of leaves flashing in wind was its anagram.
It could be stomped on by barbarians, savages, Goths.
It could sit upright on a blunt, oiled stake, be squashed by quadriplegic
elephants, and never recited by eunuchs or hermaphrodites
at weddings in India. Although invisible, its apogee was transmission.

Let it lie disemboweled in a vacant lot like a quadriplegic
Cadillac, its anagram garbled by poetically correct hermaphrodites—
the poem outlives deconstructing Goths, and its own transmission.

THE CHICHIMECAS

The Chichimecas are in the hills.
They have built a huge bonfire.
I am at my window with a telescope
counting shadows flickering in front of the flames.
There must be at least a thousand Chichimecas
and their many dogs, for they are the dog people.

Maybe there is only one Chichimeca
and his dog pacing back and forth
in front of the fire trying to make me think
that there are one thousand Chichimecas in the hills.

There are Chichimecas in the alley.
They have taken down the street signs
and built another bonfire—STOP, SCHOOL CROSSING,
SLIPPERY WHEN WET, the Chichimecas are showing
a preference for S's slithering into smoke.

The Chichimecas have broken into the abandoned
train station from one of my poems. The one
where the sound of the plastic tips of my shoelaces
clicks against pavement like lobsters.
They are cooking the lobsters in a steel drum.
After they have devoured the lobsters, they lie down
with their dogs. Sniff, sniff, sniff, sniff the dogs.

Sniff, sniff, sniff, sniff the Chichimecas,
for they have found aerosol paint cans
and they are holding rags soaked with paint spray
to their noses. This makes the moon come down.

Chichi mommy, *chichi* mommy, chant the Chichimecas
as they fall asleep in a pile with their many dogs.
Chichi mommy as they snore and dream that the stars
are dripping milk into their open mouths.

RED ROPES OF THE HOTEL EDEN

You follow red ropes that lay out a path
through the hallway of a decrepit hotel where
the walls are faded green and the carpet smells
like wet burlap. Mr. Patel, the manager, bellhop,
and maid, skitters about all afluster, bobbing,
almost hopping, the red epaulets on his shoulders
flashing like berries in a windblown bush.
You find a faded newspaper on the bed.
There is a story about you on the front page.
Something bad you did to your best friends
in a campground a long time ago with an axe.
You don't remember, hardly recognize the photo—
so young—holding a number against your chest,
blissful, perhaps the happiest you'll ever be.
But let's try another past, another present.
We'll keep the ropes. They line a street in L.A.
in what you thought was the way out of a jam
but now you realize you're caught in a line of cars
at a movie premiere. No way out but to creep
forward so you do, in your beat-up red convertible,
wearing your baseball cap, needing a shave. Thus
you're mistaken for a movie director known to drive
a beat-up red convertible, wear a baseball cap,
and seldom shave. The crowd on each side
of the red ropes begins to call out and applaud.
An actress about to cross the street recognizes you.
Obviously, she wants to be in your next picture.
She smiles, waves and starts a long-legged, undulant
stride toward you, her dress rippling with the creaminess
of a black-and-white photograph of a mountain stream.
You begin to inhale lavender with a hint of patchouli.
Is it Amouage? Is it Lumière? But she knows now

that you are not the man she thought you were.
Her upper lip, glossy and plump, arches in disdain
for your ordinariness as she turns on her heel.
You had it all for a moment: fame, polite respectful
applause—a certain nonchalance toward celebrity
and the sweet lingering pain of lost love
as she turned away from you. But let's not savor it,
let's look at an alternate take. You're with the actress
in your favorite alcove at the Brown Derby. A fifty-
dollar tip for Jimmy and he pulls the curtain, clips
the red velvet-covered rope across the opening
that signifies *do not disturb*. Close-up on the rope.
Slow dissolve, as it becomes a log in a campfire.
Over morning coffee you're telling your friends
at the campground about your dream—sleepy,
slow talking, still in the dream: you are an old man.
Just released from a hospital for the criminally insane.
Something you can't remember. The room. Mr. Patel,
who reminds you of a parakeet in a painting you vaguely
recall might have been named The Hotel Eden . . . his jumpy
twittering about . . . the newspaper on the bed . . . the red
ropes . . . the red ropes. Your friends laugh, nervously.

THE FUTURE OF THE FIFTIES

After a version of *Swan Lake* starring Daffy Duck, the Thing
clomps through the arctic substation of the Strategic Air
Command. It's only James Arness but I hide under the vinyl seat
anyway, my face pressed into the sticky gum and popcorn floor
because the Thing wants to eat the scientists, they want to kill it but
there's no stopping the doors of the 1950s from flying open, letting
in creatures from outer space, big Russians, communists in their
wire-rimmed glasses, Red Chinese hordes goose-stepping out of
the waves of the Pacific Ocean like the sudden emergence of a fatal
continent, until all the sirens ring at once and it's time to duck and
cover, time for the blossoming of the huge sphere, the giant,
transparent bubble that fits like a lid over the city, but instead of
green like Oz it's orange like fire. I'm standing on a cliff at Land's
End holding hands with a lady friend—not the one I can't quite kiss
while Prince Valiant clangs against the Black Knight, his singing sword
slicing up a grove of perfectly straight young trees, but Monica Di
Emidio, the one whose husband, unable to forget torture in Cuba,
will hang himself from the showerhead, the one whose son I'll fail
to recognize while he attends a class I'm teaching at San Quentin
prison, who'll come home at last, lie on her couch to take a nap and
die, and she'll call after all these years to ask if I can help find his
poems. But this morning in 1959 it's the blazing sky from *The War
of the Worlds*. It's that mandatory atomic dream, and when I turn
to Monica to ask her what her name is, she replies, Eve, as if I
hadn't always known it. After all, we are the ones who hold
our breath in wonder at the Haight theater, after the whirlwind,
the foreboding, the nostalgic, crisp scent of sepia, as Dorothy looks
out the door to a new, Technicolor world. We are the ones stunned
with the munchkins as we bend and stare at those long striped
stockings curling up under the farmhouse.
We are the ones who listen when told to pay no attention
to the man behind the curtain, not to stare at the flash

in the sky or to look the future of the Fifties in the face
even though it's so beautiful, now that it is finally here—
so brilliant it passes right through our bodies, pasting
our white, paper-thin shadows to the one wall left standing.

TOWHEAD

Your brother had a different father,
Mother said softly,
as if speaking to herself,
His hair was like corn silk.
Dipped in the inkwell,
my brother called me,
Your pigtails were dipped
in the inkwell
and it soaked all the way up.
He played with my dolls,
I liked his six-gun,
his cowboy shirt.
Once in a while Father
under his breath
behind his newspaper
would sigh, Damn
towheaded milkman.
At night in the treehouse
we lay side by side,
two Scotty dog magnets.
Was there a moment we
could hear the stars click,
feel the treehouse
come unmoored
before we each woke
under different stars?
He said, I'll be a bank robber,
write you a letter on the back
of a wanted poster.
Maybe he is.
Maybe he's nearby or far.
Sometimes at work, the blur

of gurneys, IVs, I think
I see a shock of blond-white
hair against a sheet
and catch my breath,
half fear, half hope.
Sometimes I'm alone
waiting in an old car
outside a bank.
He leaps in the driver's
seat, still a teenager.
We speed off.
Sirens diminish.
In the country now
we turn toward each other
and smile. Both of us
with silky, cream-colored hair.

WITH YOUR EYES CLOSED

I was asleep
while a stranger
stripped me bare,
removing my saddle shoes
my white knee-stockings
my green and black
kilt skirt in the regulation
Black Watch pattern,
and made love to me.
And as he made love to me
I was dreaming
that I poured the last
drops of my grandmother's
rarest peach brandy
down the toilet.
My grandmother
was on the front porch
rocking back and forth
in her rocker, an activity
I believe is sexual.
Then I became
my grandmother,
the chair was a huge
black stallion because
I was small again.
I clenched my thighs,
we galloped along a ridge,
the moon was full,
but cast no light because
it had become the tire
of my boyfriend's car
and I was letting

the air out while he
was in the library
somewhere in the stacks
making love to my best friend.
I have always found bookshelves
to be erotic, so I became
my best friend
but I won't tell you
her name, or mine either.
If I have learned anything
it is this: you should never
tell anyone your name
in a dream, even if you're
not really sleeping.

Missing You

You were a river stained rusty red
from the heat of one thousand volcanoes.
I was just an ashy mist rising from wet ferns.
Around the time of the Spanish Inquisition
I caught a glimpse of your eyes behind a veil.
Once, you lit a blaze in a hearth, and I
was not even wood, but the skeleton of a gnat
embedded in rosin, a brief scent released
into a room full of women writing poetry,
where a dog, asleep on a blanket, dreamt
of his former home, of the shed with its blankets,
the yard, the alley where he chased balls
with that other dog, buried bones. . . .
Many years ago I stood on a ladder
painting a house in San Francisco.
You stopped below to watch me, same eyes,
light green, knowing . . . but you
were a schoolgirl and I a full-grown man.
Tonight I'm walking alone in the park.
You have decided to make a brief appearance
as a white slash across an almost starless sky.
Did you see that? I say, as if speaking to someone.

The Party

A man wanted to invite people he had seen only in his dreams to a party. He wondered where to send the invitations.

He also wondered if there was a way to invite the many people that he had been in his dreams. Would inviting himself be adequate?

And what about those people he had seen only in his dreams? The orange minotaur, the gangsters, the Nazi colonel who played chess with him, the woman on the stepladder at the library . . . and what about the skeletons and skulls, and Raquel Welch . . . this was getting complicated.

Besides, there was really only one person he had seen only in his dreams that he wanted to invite. In fact, this whole party idea was just a ruse, what he hoped would be a kind of message, a posthypnotic suggestion that would enable him to see her again.

Maybe if he could dream of a post office, he could send the invitations. He wondered if people in his dreams had email now. Oh, and his cellmate, the man he had argued with over whose dream it was . . .

And what about the people in the background, those who set the scenes and helped out? It was no use. Maybe someone in his dreams would invite him to a party.

He would see her there. She'd be off to the side of the room, engaged in conversation, pretending not to notice his entrance. Pretending that she hadn't dreamt up this whole party idea just so she could see him again. . . .

Louie, M.D., Ph.D.

There was a dog that was a psychiatrist who wanted to analyze his master. He was aware of the ethical and professional problems analyzing his own master could create.

Regardless, because his master seemed depressed, he decided to proceed. He would sit by his master's side and wait for him to speak. But all his master ever said to him was, Sit, Come, or Stay. The dog suspected that his master was fixated on these three words.

Later he wrote in his notebook, I believe that the patient was forced to remain in a closet for long periods of time during his childhood, impairing the development of his language skills.

The dog that was a psychiatrist waited for his master to lie on the couch and talk about his childhood. But his master never lay on the couch. It was as if, the dog thought, his master was afraid of falling asleep.

So the dog would lie on the couch in comfortable-looking positions of ease. He would stretch out, close his eyes and sigh with pleasure. He would lie upside down with his paws in the air. He would make running movements with his legs to indicate he was having a pleasant, squirrel-chasing dream.

He hoped that by following this example his master would lose his fear of sleep. But all his master did was stand there offering him a Milk-Bone.

Milk, the dog later wrote in his notebook, Perhaps a reference to his mother's breasts. Bone, he wrote, Perhaps he is overcome with his fear of death.

The dog who was a psychiatrist sat in his office late into the night. He was concerned about how little progress his master was making in therapy. He stared at his notes . . . raised one ear . . . cocked his head to one side . . . chewed on his pencil. . . .

❖❖❖

Allegory of the Speed Bump

There was a man who wanted to be a speed bump. Not just any speed bump, but a speed bump that drivers would pass over slowly, with attention and appreciation. What a perfect speed bump, they would reflect. Not too big so it makes you bounce. Not so small that it might just as well not be there.

He tried lying in the street with a flattened cardboard box over his body. But the cardboard got caught in the car's wheels and fell apart after being dragged some distance. He tried placing a section of corrugated tin over his body but this was much too loud, clumping and flapping, and its sharp edges damaged the tires.

Did the man have low self-esteem? Was he a masochist? No, he was just a man who wanted to be a speed bump.

Especially at night. He imagined himself as a speed bump in a quiet residential lane. Elm trees lined the sidewalk and arched over the street. A young couple would pass ever so slowly over him. The couple were silent. They were holding hands. Perhaps they were viscerally aware of the allegory of the speed bump—the slow rise of anticipation, the almost imperceptible pause of apogee, then the slow descent, and the inevitable return to flatness.

Maybe after I retire from being a speed bump, the man thought, I could become a pause in conversation. Not the kind when you say, Someone just walked over my grave. But the pause in conversation that is beyond words, the kind where you feel a chill across the back of your neck, and the hair on your arms stands up.

THE DIAGRAM

It is in two columns. There is a zero at the top, between and above the columns. In each column, memories: a hand you once saw pressed against a foggy bus window . . . a year-and-a-half-old child calls out her version of your name in a hallway.

The zero at the top has great weight. Yet, like the creation of the universe, which was once visible on the diagram, each event continues to happen, moving forward through time, leaving behind a trace of its having happened—the way a traffic jam is the aftermath of an accident that happened hours ago.

A professor leans his pointer against the diagram, but says nothing. But you see it—yes—the resemblance of the diagram to an enormous tree. The leaves of the tree are dark green on top and light green on the underside. The zero, as it falls, sets the leaves flashing in a complicated binary of one-two, yes-no, dark-light. Of course, a message of some kind.

But this only makes you angry. You know that the diagram, its leaves pulsating, will always be beyond your understanding.

PARK IN EDINBURGH

Take a walk by the gated park in Edinburgh.
You've heard how each apartment dweller
across the street has their own key,
except for those who live in the basement
apartments, no keys for basement dwellers.
Climb the fence that's covered with lobelia,
leap off, careful not to land on the violets,
and slip between two scraggly cypresses
that are too sad to remind anyone of Italy
or of Van Gogh's flame-like cypresses.
Make your way toward the luxurious solitude
of a bench in a cul-de-sac. But what if someone
pokes their head out a window and yells,
Can I help you?—meaning, What are you doing
in our park, you stupid American? Perhaps
a gamekeeper in a checkered shirt will emerge
from one of the basement apartments
and ask you to leave. But so what?
This park is a memory, or maybe a photograph
of a memory. But then again, when you look closer
at the ivy trembling in the breeze, the park
could be a painting collapsing into blotches
and swirls of viridian and burnt sienna. You like
the soft clatter of dishes and muted conversation
from the windows. You like being outside the houses,
listening, not belonging in the park, and the way
the trees soak up gray light, as a flock
of starlings flash black and white,
an alphabet flung against the sky.

New Orleans

You're strolling hand in hand, occasional
mouth to mouth, through the French Quarter,
all *bons temps rouler*, when a one-eyed jack
gives you the *mal ojo*. So you duck into a shop
where an African mask with a corona of snake
warns you in the voice of Marie Laveau—Your wife,
she look for juju to hoodoo you. But you
don't care, you're off to the bayou, where Spanish
moss drips from banyan trees that are up
to their knees in trouble, and the pluff mud smells,
your lover says, just like childhood—sour pennies
in morning mist. Your tour guide, Mr. Magpie,
god of the crossroads, fluent in English, Creole,
French, Gullah, walks by your side. He of the frock coat.
Tiny preacher, hands behind his back—talk to him,
he'll listen, head cocked to one side, nodding.

MOTEL 6, PADUCAH, KENTUCKY

The Motel 6 sign extinguishes any stars
attempting to glow in its radiance.
But only the moon can be the moon
on this night of crickets, magnolias,
the asphyxiated gurgling of a small stream,
the clacking of a freight train along its infinite ladder.

That's us strolling beneath the embankment
with our dog in the parking lot of Motel 6
where the clicking of the crickets is dark green,
and the marble coolness of your shoulder is nostalgic
like a song from the 1920s.
Even our dog knows we are in Paducah,

as he rolls over on his back in the damp grass
thinking *I am in Paducah*
not quite understanding what that means
but liking the sound of the word, and I
like it too, Paducah, Paducah, the ways it mimics
the waltzing pulse of the freight train.

And why not ponder the meaning of 6
thrown against the universe
like a card on a velvet table?
The inverse power of nine, you and I,
the moon, Motel 6 sign, little stream,
the train fading into the night, our dog—

or are we just a perfect copy that has
no original, only dreaming that we're dreaming?
Ooo eee, ooo ah ah, ting tang, walla walla bing bang

tumbles out of someone's radio
and lightning rattles its witchdoctor bones
illuminating darkness like a crime scene.

The Motel 6 sign scrapes a couple of stars
out of the sky. Curious, Mars leans so near,
I think it's a police helicopter. El Romantico,
that's me, holds you closer. Listen—six Motel 6 signs
in a row and the six angels of revelation
shall blow mightily on six silver trumpets.

These are the words of the Motel 6 sign.
No, these are the words of the moon.

ACKNOWLEDGMENTS

Grateful acknowledgment is made to the editors of the following print and online journals, in which these poems appeared, sometimes in slightly different form or with different titles:

Bat City Review: "The Persistence of Objects";

Beyond Baroque: "Red Ropes of the Hotel Eden";

Blackbird: "Ashes of Roses";

The Blue Moon Review: "The Blueness";

Crazyhorse: "Autumn";

Colorado Review: "If Only";

The Cortland Review: "Colorado," "With Your Eyes Closed";

Court Green: "The Future of the Fifties";

Crab Orchard Review: "Opportunities";

Double Room: "Shoes," "The Party";

Ecotone: "Those Moments";

88: "Hollywood," "Not Bad for a Hermaphrodite";

Hayden's Ferry Review: "Considering Your Hand";

Illuminations: "Self-Portrait as Goya";

Indiana Review: "My Father's Hands";

Kestrel: "Ghazal of the Laundromat," "Nick of Time," "The Chichimecas";

Knock: "The Element of Water";

Los Angeles Poetry Festival—Noir Corridor: "Angel Face";

Luna: "Pavilions Motel," "Ponce de León and the Ten Milkshakes," "Queen of the Night";

Midwest Review: "Dark Passage," "Not His Room";

Notre Dame Review: "Adam and Eve's Dog," "My Mother and Your Mother," "The Peaceable Kingdom";

New Southerner: "Motel 6, Paducah, Kentucky";

nthposition: "Funhouse Mirror," "Me and Nash," "Explosions";

Perihelion: "Louie, M.D., Ph.D.," "My Father's False Teeth";

Pool: "Miracles," "Mozart's Concerto for Glass Harmonica";

Quarterly West: "New Orleans," "Sewers of Charleston";

Sentence: "The Allegory of the Speed Bump," "The Diagram," "The Violet Vale";

Slope: "The Brochure," "The Moon";

Solo: "Richard Garcia Steals a Poem";

"Adam and Eve's Dog" appears in *Best American Poetry 2005, ed.* Paul Muldoon (Scribner Poetry, 2005); "Nick of Time" and "Richard Garcia Steals a Poem" appear in *Beyond the Valley of the Contemporary Poets 2000 Anthology*, ed. by Brendan Constantine and Amélie Frank (VCP Press, 2001); "Dreaming of Sheena" appears in *Blue Arc West: An Anthology of California Poets*, ed. Paul Suntup (TebotBach, 2005); "Angel Face," "Ghazal of the Laundromat," and "Richard Garcia Steals a Poem" appear in *The Brink: An Anthology of Postmodern Poetry from 1965 to the Present*, ed. Noah Hoffenberg (Yeti Books, 2002); "Angel Face," "Dark Passage," and "Richard Garcia Steals a Poem" appear in *Inscape 2002*, ed. Department of English, Pasadena City College, 2002; "My Father's Hands" appears in *Family Matters: Poems of Our Families*, ed. Ann & Larry Smith (Bottom Dog Press, 2005); "Crepuscule in Blue or Green" appears in *Mischief, Caprice, and Other Poetic Strategies*, ed. Terry Wolverton (Red Hen Press, 2002); "Furry Lewis Drops in on Surrealism 101" appears in *So Luminous the Wildflowers: An Anthology of California Poets*, ed. Paul Suntup (Tebot Bach, 2003).

"The Blue Dress" contains quotes from *Chicken, Shadow, Moon and More* by Mark Strand, published by Turtle Point Press. "Miracles" contains quotes from *Memoirs of My Nervous Illness* by Daniel Paul Schreber, published by New York Review of Books Classics. "The Truth of Morning" and "How Many" contain quotes from *One Hundred Love Sonnets* by Pablo Neruda, published by University of Texas Press.

❖❖❖

ABOUT THE AUTHOR

Richard Garcia was born in San Francisco in 1941 to a Puerto Rican father and Mexican mother. His previous books of poetry include *The Flying Garcias* from the University of Pittsburgh Press and *Rancho Notorious* from BOA Editions. He holds a Master of Fine Arts degree from the Warren Wilson Program for Writers. He has won many awards for his work, including a Pushcart Prize and fellowships from the National Endowment for the Arts, the California Arts Council, and the Cohen Award from *Ploughshares*. For twelve years he was Poet-in-Residence at Children's Hospital in Los Angeles, where he conducted poetry and art workshops for hospitalized children. He teaches in the Antioch University Los Angeles MFA Low Residency Program and is on the teaching staff of the Idyllwild Poetry Festival. He lives with his wife Katherine Williams and their dog Louie on James Island, South Carolina, where he conducts private workshops at home and online.

❖❖❖

BOA Editions, Ltd.: American Poets Continuum Series

COLOPHON

The Persistence of Objects, poems by Richard Garcia,
is set in Centaur, a digitalized version of the font designed
for Monotype by Bruce Rogers in 1928.
The italic, based on drawings by Frederic Warde,
is an interpretation of the work of the sixteenth-century printer
and calligapher Ludovico degli Arrighi, after whom it is named.

❖ ❖ ❖

The publication of this book is made possible, in part,
by the special support of the following individuals:

Jeanne Marie Beaumont
Alan & Nancy Cameros
Gwen & Gary Conners
Burch & Louise Craig
Susan K. Dunn
Bev & Pete French
Dane & Judy Gordon
Kip & Deb Hale
Peter & Robin Hursh
Robert & Willy Hursh
Archie & Pat Kutz
Rosemary & Lew Lloyd
John & Barbara Lovenheim
Jimmy & Wendy Mnookin
Boo Poulin
Pat & Michael Wilder
Glenn & Helen William

❖ ❖ ❖